A Visit to

The Police Station

Revised Edition

4D

Download the
Capstone 4D app
for additional content.

See page 2
for directions.

by Patricia J. Murphy

CAPSTONE PRESS
a capstone imprint

Download the Capstone 4D app!

- Ask an adult to search in the Apple App Store or Google Play for "Capstone 4D".
- Click Install (Android) or Get, then Install (Apple).
- Open the app.
- Scan any of the following spreads with this icon:

When you scan a spread, you'll find fun extra stuff to go with this book!
You can also find these things on the web at www.capstone4D.com
using the password: **police.08314**

Pebble Plus is published by Capstone Press,
1710 Roe Crest Drive, North Mankato, Minnesota 56003
www.mycapstone.com

Library of Congress Cataloging-in-Publication Data
is available on the Library of Congress website.

ISBN 978-1-5435-0831-4 (library binding)
ISBN 978-1-5435-0843-7 (paperback)
ISBN 978-1-5435-0871-0 (ebook pdf)

Editorial Credits
Sarah Bennett, designer; Tracy Cummins, media researcher;
Laura Manthe, production specialist

Photo Credits
Alamy: David R. Frazier Photolibrary Inc, 19, keith morris, 11;
Capstone Press: Gary Sundermeyer, 5, 9, 13, 17, 21, Jim Foell, 3,
15; Capstone Studio: Karon Dubke, Cover Background, Cover
Left; Shutterstock: amirage, Design Element, Photographee.eu, 7

Note to Parents and Teachers

The A Visit to set supports national social studies standards
related to the production, distribution, and consumption of
goods and services. This book describes and illustrates a police
station. The images support early readers in understanding the
text. The repetition of words and phrases helps early readers
learn new words. This book also introduces early readers to
subject-specific vocabulary words, which are defined in the
Glossary section. Early readers may need assistance to read
some words and to use the Table of Contents, Glossary, Read
More, Internet Sites, Critical Thinking Questions, and Index
sections of the book.

Printed in the United States of America.
010767S18

Table of Contents

The Police Station

A police station is a place
where police officers work.
Police officers help
keep communities safe.

5

People report accidents
and crimes at the station.
They ask police officers
for help.

Dispatchers answer
emergency calls.
They send police officers
to help people.

Police Officers

Police officers check in
before starting their shifts.
The watch commander gives
them jobs at roll call.

Police officers drive squad cars.
The cars have lights
and sirens.

Some officers work with dogs.

The dogs help officers

investigate crimes.

Officers take fingerprints
and mug shots.

They interview suspects.

Around the Station

Police stations have cells.

Each cell has a bed,

a sink, and a toilet.

A police station is
busy day and night.
It is always open.

21

Glossary

cell—a small room with locks; some cells have bars

dispatcher—a person who answers 911 calls and assigns rescue workers

interview—to ask questions about something important

investigate—to find out as much as possible about an event or a person

shift—a set number of hours that a person works

suspect—a person who may be responsible for a crime

Read More

Best, B. J. *Police Cars.* Riding to the Rescue! New York: Cavendish Square Publishing, 2018.

Murray, Julie. *The Police Station.* My Community: Places. Minneapolis: Abdo Kids, 2017.

Siemens, Jared. *Police Officer.* People in My Neighborhood. New York: Smartbook Media Inc., 2018.

Internet Sites

Use FactHound to find Internet sites related to this book.

Visit *www.facthound.com*

Just type **9781543508314** and go.

 Check out projects, games and lots more at
www.capstonekids.com

Critical Thinking Questions

1. What does a dispatcher do?

2. Describe what a police officer does.

3. Why is a police station an important place in a community?

Index